5 Minute Edible Crafts:

A Family Cookbook for Kids

Wolf Cub Chlo

5 Minute Edible Crafts

A FAMILY COOKBOOK

for Kids

40+ fun recipes for kids plus **FREE** bonuses inside

Wolf Cub Chlo

FREE GIFTS

Get ready for a summer full of delicious treats and unforgettable moments with our exclusive **Fun Summer Activity Guide** and **Bonus Recipe Pack**

Inside, you will discover:

- **Bonus recipe pack** featuring additional family-friendly, creative, and mouthwatering smoothies, popsicles, milkshakes, ice cream cookies, and more.
- **Fun Summer Activity Guide:** Screen-Free Entertainment that encourages: Fun Outdoor Games, Entertaining crafts, Nature exploration, Social Skill Development, and much more

If you want to create endless fun and scrumptious delights all summer long, grab your free bonuses today!

~~$47 Value~~ FREE

To the little and
big chefs
that love making
art out of their
food,

the world is your
stencil.

Contents

Note to grown-up chefs

Here's a fun, simple way to bond with your children safely in the kitchen that doesn't involve screen time and can still count as being productive.

My daughter and I have found that cooking together is a way to be creative, read, bond, and have fun all at the same time.

We are sharing the formula to help you do the same in this fun cookbook for kids series.

Here's what you will find in the book:
- **FREE BONUS**: The ultimate shopping list that gives you access to everything you need before even getting started, coloring pages, and fun food trivia.
- Silly jokes for kids for extra giggles
- Fun facts with every recipe
- Simple and fun food craft recipes that the entire family can participate in.
- Fun recipe names (similar beginning sounds, similar ending sounds, or easy-to-pronounce sounds.)
- **BONUS Fun Activity Section**

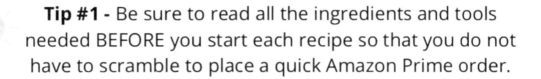

Tip #1 - Be sure to read all the ingredients and tools needed BEFORE you start each recipe so that you do not have to scramble to place a quick Amazon Prime order.

Tip #2 - These recipes are simple but not intended for kids to do by themselves; rather, they were created with the intention of being a fun activity that can be done together as a family or with friends. This takes the guesswork out of your next activity and gives you an easy way to bond as a unit

Tip #3: The goal is not to strive for perfection, but increase creativity. So let your imagination run wild and allow the kids to do the same as well.

Tip #4: These recipes can also be done strictly by you, the grown-up, for special breakfast occasions, after-school afternoon snacks, lunchbox surprises, and desserts. They are also great to use for kid parties, small get-togethers, family game nights, baby showers, gift exchanges, and more. So let the fun and the baking commence! Enjoy!

Enjoy simple Recipe crafts that are not intimidating, but fun! The sillier the recipe turns out, the more laughs you will get, which will allow you to spend more time enjoying the art of playing and creating with your food and less time being frustrated by the outcome of the recipe.

Jenn aka Mama Wolf

Note to kid chefs

Raise your hand if you are ready to play with your food and have some fun!

I love playing with my food, creating fun recipes, and having lots of fun. In fact, there are fun silly jokes and cool fun facts for you with every recipe.

Before we start, here are some quick safety tips:
- Make sure you work with a grown-up to be extra safe while having fun.
- Always wash your hands before touching food.
- Wash all fruits and veggies with a grown-up before eating them.
- Read ingredients to double-check for food allergies.
- Clean up your workstation as you go so that you are not stuck cleaning later.
- Read directions carefully. Grown-up knives should be handled by grown-ups and kid knives can be handled by you.

Now that we've got all the boring stuff away, it's time to get baking. So, let's have some FUN!

Chloé aka Wolf Cub Chlo

Fruit Snack Crafts

INGREDIENTS

- 1 orange
- 1 blueberry
- 2 candy eyes

TOOLS

- Grown-up knife
- Cutting board
- Long rectangular plate

Fun Fact:
A dog's sense of smell is 40x stronger than humans.

Orange Puppy

 2 servings   5 minutes

Joke:

What do you call a cold dog?

Chili dog

1. Arrange one orange slice on top of the plate and another directly underneath (head and body).
2. Next, take another slice and lay it directly on top of both slices (snout).
3. Arrange candy eyes above the snout.
4. Cut large blueberry in half and place one-half down (nose).
5. Slice the other blueberry half into 3 small pieces to be used as the eyebrows and mouth.
6. Attach 2 orange halves on either side of the head (ears).
7. Cut out thin rectangles from the orange rind (legs and tail).

Isn't your puppy the cutest?

INGREDIENTS

- Half pear (sliced vertically
- Approx. 20 grapes
- Approx.15 blueberries
- 2 candy eyes
- Baby carrot

TOOLS

- Grown-up knife
- Long plate

Peacock Pear Paradise

(Try saying that three times really fast.)

🍴 3 servings   🕐 5 minutes

Tongue Twister:

The peacock picked a pickled piping pepper.

1. Cut the pear in half vertically and place on plate. Then add both candy eyes to the center of the pear.
2. Arrange 2 layers of grapes and blueberries around the pear.
3. Place one small carrot shred under the eyes (beak).
4. Add 3 small carrot shreds under the pear on the left and right side (feet).

🙂

Fun Fact:

Only males are called peacocks and have the most vibrant colors; females are called peahens.

INGREDIENTS

- 2 celery sticks
- 16 candy eyes
- Grapes
- Cucumber slices
- Strawberry slices
- Cherry tomatoes
- Peanut butter

(or butter substitute)

TOOLS

- kid-safe knife

Busy Bug Celery Sticks

 8 servings   5 minutes

Joke:

How do bugs send letters to their friends? By using snail mail.

1. Cut each celery stick into 4 pieces.
2. Use a kid-friendly butter knife to spread the peanut butter on each celery stick.
3. Arrange grapes, cucumber slices, strawberries, and cherry tomatoes on each celery stick.
4. Add 2 small candy eyes in front of each "bug."

Bug appétit!

Fun Fact:

Have you heard of stink bugs? Stink bugs are native to Asia and become super stinky when they are scared, threatened, crushed, or when trying to attract another stink bug.

INGREDIENTS

- 1 large orange
- Blueberries
- Green apples
- Carrots

TOOLS

- Grown-up knife

Fun Fact:

Chickens are not vegetarians; they are omnivores. They eat grass, grain, lizards, insects, and mice.

Chick Chat Oranges

 2 servings   5 minutes

Joke:

What do chickens call bowling balls?

Eggrolls

1. Cut the orange into 5 slices.
2. Place two slices, one on top of the other, on one side of the plate (head and body).
3. Set one blueberry inside the top orange slice (eye).
4. Place an orange half on an angle on the body (wing).
5. Add 3 thin carrot strips at the bottom (feet).
6. Place two strips on the side of the head (beak).
7. Use green apples to decorate the bottom of the plate (grass blades)
8. Repeat for the additional chick.

Enjoy

INGREDIENTS

- 1 kiwi
- 12 grapes

TOOLS

- Toothpicks
- Grown-up knife/potato peeler

Fun Fact:

The hawksbill sea turtle may have been on earth for over 100 million years. They are sadly considered a critically endangered species now.

Kiwi Turtle Grapes

 3 servings   5 minutes

Joke:

How do turtles communicate?

With their shell-phones.

1. Peel the kiwi and cut into 3 medium-sized slices.

2. Push one toothpick horizontally across the front and another toothpick into the back of the kiwi.

3. Cut one grape in half and place each half on the left side of the toothpick. Repeat the same step for the right side of the toothpick (feet).

4. Push another toothpick from front to back and set one grape at the head of the vertical toothpick (head).

5. Cut another grape in half and place it at the opposite end of the turtle (tail).

6. Repeat for the remaining kiwi slices.

Turtle power!

INGREDIENTS

- 1 green apple
- 3 blueberries
- 1 kiwi

TOOLS

- Grown-up knife
- Cutting board

Fun Fact:

Bears are omnivores; they eat meat and vegetables, but they love honey.

They can weigh 60 pounds (27kg) - 1600 pounds (725 kg)!

Bear Apples

 1 serving 5 minutes

Tongue Twister:

A big black bug bit a big black bear.

1. Cut and pit green apple into a ½ inch (1.27 cm) thick slice.
2. Next, arrange two blueberries (eyes).
3. Peel and cut the kiwi slice into a semi-circle and place under the eyes (nose).
4. Set blueberry on top of the kiwi slice (nostril).
5. Place two semi-circle kiwi slices above the eyes (ears).

You are ready for a bear-y adventurous snack!

INGREDIENTS

- 4 bread slices
- Banana
- Green apple (half)
- Orange (half)

TOOLS

- Grown-up knife
- Long plate

Banana Palm Tree

 2 servings  5 minutes

Joke:

What kind of tree should fit in your

hand? A palm tree.

1. Slice the entire banana and place on a rectangular plate (tree trunk).
2. Slice the entire apple half and arrange above banana (leaves).
3. Slice the orange and set a few slices at the base of the banana (sand).
4. Place the final slice at the top corner of the plate (sun).

Fun Fact:

Over one million earths can fit

inside the sun.

INGREDIENTS

- 1 orange
- 2 cucumbers
- 2 blueberries
- 1 baby carrot

TOOLS

- Grown-up knife

Fun Fact:

There are over 600 varieties of Oranges. Also, the orange color was named after the fruit.

Cheery Chick Orange

 1 serving   5 minutes

Joke:

Why did the orange need glasses?

He needed Vitamin See.

1. Cut the orange into two slices and place one above the other (head and body).

2. Cut two more orange slices and place on either side of the bottom of the orange (wings).

3. Place two cucumber slices on top of the orange slice (eyes).

4. Place 2 blueberries in the center of each cucumber (pupils).

5. Shred the baby carrot into thin slices and place two tiny shreds above the orange slice (hair).

6. Place one long shred and two smaller shreds at the base of the second orange (foot). Repeat for the second foot.

"Orange" you glad you can finally eat?

INGREDIENTS

- 2 orange slices
- 1 tsp. of chia seeds
- 6 banana chunks
- 2 grapes
- 2 colored straws cut in half

TOOLS

- Grown-up knife

Fun Fact:

There are over 8,000 grape varieties. One cup of grapes gives more than enough Vitamin K and C needed for the day.

Rain Cloud Orange Umbrella

 1 serving   5 minutes

Riddle:

Why did the man stare at the orange juice container? Because it said to concentrate.

UMBRELLA

1. Cut the orange into slices and place on the plate (umbrella).
2. Place colored straw halves directly under the orange slices (handle).

RAIN AND CLOUDS

3. Scatter the chia seeds along the umbrella (rain).
4. Place banana chunks above each umbrella (clouds).

CATERPILLAR

5. Slice two grapes in half and place below the umbrellas.

(Optional: use two green sprinkles for antennas and 2 candy eyes for eyes).

INGREDIENTS

- 6 strawberries
- 12 large candy eyes
- 6 yellow chocolate candies
- Small handful milk chocolate melting wafers

TOOLS

- Kid-safe knife
- Microwavable bowl

Strawberry Penguins

 2 servings   5 minutes

Riddle:

I can be red or green.

I get grown on a vine.

I'm dried to make raisins.

Or squeezed to help make wine.

What am I?

Riddle Answer: Grapes

1. Melt milk chocolate wafers in a microwave at 20-second intervals. Watch carefully.

2. Caution: Hot! Dip the tip of each strawberry into the chocolate.

3. Place 2 candy eyes on top of each strawberry (they will stick because chocolate dries up very quickly).

4. Turn the yellow chocolate candy vertically and push it into the strawberry under the eyes.

Fun Fact:

The average strawberry has over 200 seeds.

INGREDIENTS

- 1 apple
- 1 tsp. cream cheese
- 1 tsp. hazelnut spread
- 1 tsp of peanut butter (or any butter substitute)
- Optional toppings: sprinkles, raisins, mini chocolate chips, etc.

TOOLS

- Grown-up knife

Apple Donuts

 3 servings   5 minutes

Joke:

What did the donut say to the spider? DONUT come close to me.

1. Turn the apple on its side and cut it into circular slices.
2. Cut the core in the shape of a circle.
3. Spread the hazelnut, cream cheese, and peanut butter on each slice.
4. Add toppings of choice and Donut forget to enjoy!

Fun Fact:

Donuts didn't always have holes in the center. They were originally small fried balls of dough.

INGREDIENTS

- 1 banana
- Foam-canned whipping cream
- 4 strawberries
- 1 tbsp. milk chocolate melting wafers
- Sprinkles

TOOLS

- Grown-up knife

Fun Fact:
Banana skins are used to treat insect bites.

Mini Winter Banana Bites

 2 servings 5 minutes

Joke:
What happened when the fruit won a gold medal? They went bananas!

1. Place a sheet of parchment paper onto the metal sheet pan.
2. Set milk chocolate wafers in a bowl and melt in the microwave at 20-second intervals. Watch closely. Mix well.
3. Scatter the sprinkles onto a small plate.
4. Cut banana into four pieces.
5. <u>Caution: Hot!</u> Dip the bottom of the banana into melted chocolate. Roll onto sprinkles and set on paper.
6. Add whipping cream on top of the banana piece and place sliced strawberry on top.

This snack is the best of the bunch!

INGREDIENTS

- 4 toothpicks
- 12 cheddar cheese cubes
- 8 thin pretzel sticks
- 4 grape halves

TOOLS

- 4 toothpicks
- Black edible marker

Cheddar Robots

 2 servings   🕐 5 minutes

Knock knock.

Who's there?

Ann.

Ann, who?

An-droid

1. Push 3 cheddar cubes into the toothpick.
2. Draw a face in front of the cube.
3. Place half of a grape on top of the robot head.
4. Push thin Pretzel sticks on both sides of the robot (arms).

Eat before your robot gets rusty.

Fun Fact:

The most popular cheese recipe in America is macaroni and cheese.

INGREDIENTS

- Baby carrot
- Grapes
- 1 strawberry
- 1 cherry tomato
- Kiwi half
- Orange bell pepper shreds
- 2 candy eyes

TOOLS

- Grown-up knife

Crab Attack Sea Snack

 1 serving   3 minutes

Joke:

Why didn't the crab share her gifts?

Because she was shell-fish.

CRAB

1. Cut the strawberry in half and place it downward on a plate. Then add candy eyes (head).
2. Cut the baby carrot into small strips and use thin baby carrots (legs).
3. Cut a small triangular piece of grape and split slightly open on top of the two carrot legs. (claws).
4. Cut the kiwi into small pieces and place under the crab (sea plants).

Enjoy Your Clawsome snack!

Fun Fact:

Crabs have 10 legs and usually walk sideways. Females can release up to 2000 eggs at a time.

INGREDIENTS

- 1 cucumber (half)
- 1 tomato (half)
- Orange bell pepper

TOOLS

- Grown-up knife
- Toothpicks

Set Sail- Sliced Cucumber Tomato Boats

 2 servings 5 minutes

Joke:

Why do ice cream scoops always carry an umbrella? Because there's always a chance of sprinkles.

1. Slice cucumber and tomatoes. Push a toothpick into cucumber slices and connect to the tomatoes.

2. Cut orange bell pepper into tiny triangles and attach to the top of each toothpick (flag).

Your snack is ready to sail the seven seas! Enjoy.

Fun Fact:

Some of the youngest sailors to sail the world were girls.

The term "feeling blue " originated at sea.

- 1 green apple
- 10 blueberries

TOOLS

- Grown-up knife

Fun Fact:

Pandas spend most of their day eating. They will eat mostly bamboo for 10-16 hours a day!

Apple Bamboo Panda

 2 servings   5 minutes

Joke:

Why did the panda upgrade their tv?

Because it was in Black and White.

1. Slice green apple into 3 medium-sized pieces and core.
2. Ser two slices on plate, one under the other (head and body).
3. Place two blueberries above the top apple slice (ears).
4. Set two blueberries inside the top apple slice (eyes).
5. Place additional blueberry under the eyes (nose).
6. Slice another blueberry into thin pieces and place as two "u- shapes" under the nose (mouth).
7. Place four remaining blueberries inside the bottom slice; two at the top and two at the bottom (arms and legs).
8. Use the remaining apple to decorate as bamboo leaves.

INGREDIENTS

- Orange slice
- 2 baby carrots
- 3 purple grapes
- 4 green grapes
- 2 small candy eyes

TOOLS

- Grown-up knife

Buzzing Butterfly and Caterpillar Grapes

 1 serving 3 minutes

Joke:

Why do caterpillars love to party?

Because they are social butterflies.

BUTTERFLY

1. Cut grapes in half and place next to each other.

2. Add a thin strip of greenery (cucumber, spinach, kale, etc.) and place above the butterfly (antennas).

CATERPILLAR

3. Cut the purple grape in half and place on the bottom of the plate.

4. Cut green grapes in half. Place directly behind the purple grape one behind the other.

(Optional: Add spinach or mixed greens under the caterpillar.)

Buzzing Butterfly and Caterpillar Grapes Cont'd

SUN

5. Set the orange slice on the top corner of the plate.

6. Slice the baby carrot into thin strips and place it around the perimeter of the sun.

Keep your dish from fluttering away. Enjoy!

Fun Fact:

There are over 20,000 species of Butterflies. They actually have four wings—not two—and their wings are transparent.

FUN FOOD TRIVIA:

There are how many different varieties of grapes

A. 25,000

B. 16,000,000

C. 8,000

Answer: C. 8,000

Buzzing Butterfly and Caterpillar Grapes Cont'd

Directions: Draw all the insects you might see on a beautiful sunny day.

INGREDIENTS

- 1 large orange
- 9 blueberries
- 3 candy eyes
- 1 baby carrot

TOOLS

- Grown-up knife

Goldfish Orange Swim Slices

 1 serving   3 minutes

Joke:

What do goldfish eat when they are celebrating? Fish cakes.

1. Place 3 orange slices horizontally on a plate.
2. Add one candy eye to each slice.
3. Stack 3 blueberries diagonally in front of the fish (air bubbles).
4. Place two baby carrot halves behind each slice (tail).

Just keep swimming and enjoy!

Fun Fact:

There are over 30,000 different species of fish.

INGREDIENTS

- Bagel (or English Muffin)
- Cream cheese
- 3 strawberries
- 2 blueberries
- 2 mini chocolate chips

TOOLS

- Grown-up knife
- Kid-safe knife

Fun Fact:
Did you know there is an orange ladybug? They are larger than red ladybugs and also more aggressive.

Orange Winged Butterfly

 1 servings   3 minutes

Knock knock.
Who's there?
Orange
Orange who
Orange you going to open the door?

1. Arrange 4 big grapes at the center of the plate.
2. Cut the orange into slices.
3. Arrange each slice at an angle on each side of the grapes. (Wings)
4. Place each candy eye on the first grape.
5. Finally let a grown-up use a sharp knife to cut and place 2 small carrot pieces above the head (antennae)

There's nothing better than a peel-y great snack! Enjoy!

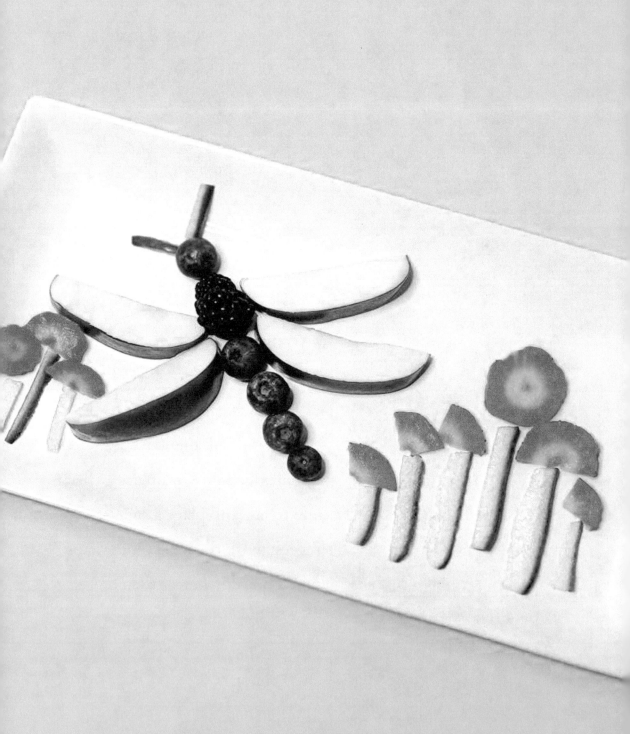

INGREDIENTS

- 1 blackberry
- 1 apple half
- 4-5 blueberries
- 2 strawberries
- Cucumber shreds

TOOLS

- Grown-up knife

Fun Fact:

Dragonflies come in a variety of colors and are some of the fastest flying insects on earth; they can even fly backward.

Blueberry Dragonfly Garden

 2 servings   3 minutes

Joke:

What's an insect's favorite subject at school? Moth-amatics!

1. Arrange one blueberry on top of a plate. (head)
2. Add blackberry and the remaining blueberries directly underneath. (body)
3. Angle two apple slices on either side of the dragonfly .(wings)
4. Arrange 2 thin cucumber pieces above the head (antennas).
5. Arrange the remaining shreds at the bottom of the plate (flower stems).
6. Cut strawberries into small slices and set on the stems (flower heads).

Voila! Enjoy your garden snack.

Apple Racers

 4 servings 5 minutes

INGREDIENTS

- 1/2 red apple
- 1/2 green apple
- 3 green grapes
- 3 purple grapes

TOOLS

- Grown-up knife
- Toothpicks

Joke:

What's a sheep's favorite type of car? Lamborghini.

1. Use an adult knife to divide the red apple into 3 slices (cars)
2. Push one toothpick vertically in the front and back of the apple slice.
3. Cut one red grape in half and attach to the exposed toothpicks on the left and right sides of the apple (wheels).
4. Repeat all the steps above with the green apple slices.

Buckle up and enjoy the fruit ride!

Fun Fact:

A top race car can reach speeds of 300 mph in 3 seconds!

Apple Racers cont'd

Directions: Help the race car driver to the finish line.

Finish

Crackers, Pretzels, & Waffle Crafts

INGREDIENTS

- 16 thin pretzel sticks
- 8 crackers
- 8 small candy eyes
- Cream cheese

TOOLS

- Kid-safe knife

Spider Cracker Attack

 4 servings 5 minutes

Joke:

How do bugs send letters to their friends? By using snail mail.

1. Use a kid-friendly knife to spread the cream cheese on the 4 crackers.
2. Lay 4 thin pretzel sticks across the cream cheese crackers.
3. Take each cracker and lay it on top of the pretzels.
4. Add 2 candy eyes for each spider. Enjoy your crawly snack!

Fun Fact:

Peacock spiders are native to Australia, about the size of a grain of rice, and love to dance.

INGREDIENTS

- Bagel (or English Muffin)
- Cream cheese
- 3 strawberries
- 2 blueberries
- 2 mini chocolate chips

TOOLS

- Grown-up knife
- Kid-safe knife

Blueberry Cracker Monster

 2 servings 3 minutes

Tongue Twister:
A big blue bucket of berry blue blueberries.

1. Take a small handful of blueberries (approx. 15) and put in a small cup.
2. Use a kid-friendly knife to spread cream cheese on 2 crackers and place them on top of the cup.
3. Take two additional blueberries and place on top of the crackers (eyes).
4. Finally, slide the last cracker halfway inside the cracker.

Fun Fact:
One single blueberry bush can produce up to 6,000 blueberries in one year!

INGREDIENTS

- Graham crackers
- Peanut butter
- Green chocolate candies
- Yellow chocolate candies
- Red chocolate candies

TOOLS

- Kid-safe knife

BONUS TIP:
Peanut butter can easily be substituted with almond butter or any other fun spread you desire.

Traffic Light Graham Crackers

 3 servings    2 minutes

Joke:

What did the red light say to the green light?

Don't look, I'm changing.

1. Spread peanut butter on the graham cracker
2. Add red, yellow, and green chocolate candies.

Green light means go. Enjoy!

Fun Fact:

Garrett Morgan was the inventor of the traffic light in 1923.

INGREDIENTS

- 1 Graham cracker
- 1 tsp. hazelnut spread
- 3 banana slices
- 2 thin pretzel sticks
- 2 mini chocolate chips
- 2 standard chocolate chips
- 1 orange sprinkle

TOOLS

- Kid-safe knife

Snowman Graham Crackers

 1 serving   2 minutes

Joke:

Why are snowmen popular? Because they are so cool.

1. Spread hazelnut across the cracker, then place 3 slices of banana, one under the other.
2. Place two mini chocolate chips on the first slice (eyes) and an orange sprinkle under eyes.
3. Next, add a standard chocolate chip onto the second and third slices (buttons).
4. Place thin pretzel sticks on both sides of the cracker (arms).

Your snowman is so cool. Enjoy

Fun Fact:

Graham crackers were created about 200 years ago by Sylvester Graham.

INGREDIENTS

- 3 chocolate Graham crackers
- 3 chocolate colored candies
- 6 candy eyes
- 6 mini pretzel twists

Chocolate Deer Crossing

 3 servings  3 minutes

Joke:

Which type of deer should always carry an umbrella? A rain deer.

1. Turn the graham crackers sideways so that they look diamond-shaped.
2. Next, arrange 2 candy eyes in the center of the deer.
3. Add two pretzels above the eyes. (horns)
4. Place one colored chocolate candy at the tip of the cracker. (nose)

Fun Fact:

There are over 40 species of deer; they are herbivores and strong swimmers.

INGREDIENTS

- 3 chocolate Graham crackers
- 6 goldfish-shaped crackers
- Green sprinkles
- Red sprinkles
- White sprinkles
- Vanilla frosting
- Light blue food coloring

TOOLS

- Grown-up knife
- Kid-safe knife

Fun Fact:

Seahorses are the only animals in which the male, not female, give birth and care for their young.

Under the Sea Graham Crackers

 2 servings   3 minutes

Knock knock,

Who's there?

Water?

Water, who?

Water you waiting for? Please open the door.

1. Mix 1 tsp of white frosting with 2 drops of food coloring. Mix well.

2. Use a kid-friendly knife to apply the spread across the bottom half of the cracker (ocean).

3. Arrange two goldfish crackers on the blue frosting.

4. Add white sprinkles (bubbles).

5. Next, add green sprinkles along the bottom of the cracker (sea plants).

6. Finally, arrange red sprinkles in the shape of a crab.

INGREDIENTS

- 6 mini pretzels
- 12 candy eyes
- 2 tbsp. white chocolate melting wafers

TOOLS

- Bowl
- Fork
- Parchment paper
- Sheet pan

Pretzel Surprise Faces

 3 servings 3 minutes

Tongue Twister:
Picky pretzel people picked perfect pretzels.

1. Align a sheet of parchment paper onto sheet pan.

2. <u>Caution: Hot</u>! Melt a small handful of chocolate melting wafers in the microwave in 20 seconds intervals.

3. <u>Caution: Hot!</u> Use a fork to dip pretzels into the chocolate and place on parchment paper.

4. Add candy eyes onto pretzels. Surpise!

Fun Fact:
Pretzels without salt are called "baldies."
National Pretzel Day in the U.S. is April 26th.

INGREDIENTS

- 1 banana
- 1 waffle

TOOLS

- Kid-safe knife

Fun Fact:

The original ingredient used in marshmallows (sap from mallow root) was used in Europe and Asia to treat sore throats.

Banana Ice Cream Waffles

 2 servings   🕐 5 minutes

Joke:

Why do ice cream scoops always carry an umbrella? Because there's always a chance of sprinkles.

1. Toast the waffle.

2. Cut the waffle down the middle at an angle.

3. Trim each piece into the shape of a triangle and arrange them onto a plate

4. Slice the banana into thin pieces and arrange as "ice cream scoops" on top of the waffle.

5. Optional: Drizzle syrup or hazelnut spread over the waffles. You can also add strawberries and other fruit for healthy decor.

Just add the cherry on top and enjoy!

INGREDIENTS

- 3 waffles
- Peanut butter (hazelnut spread or substitute butter)
- 1 milk chocolate melting wafer
- 6 standard chocolate chips
- 2 large candy eyes
- 2 red chocolate candies
- 2 small apple strips

TOOLS

- Kid-safe knife

Beaver Believer Waffle

 3 servings 5 minutes

Joke:

What's a beaver's favorite type of chips? Wood chips.

1. Spread peanut butter (or a substitute spread) onto the waffles and place one waffle above the other.

HEAD:

2. Use two chocolate chips and place them on top edge of the waffle (ears).

3. Set two candy eyes in the center of the waffle.

4. Put a milk chocolate wafer under the eyes (nose).

5. Use 2 apple strips under the chocolate wafer (teeth).

6. Set red chocolate candies on the opposite sides of the wafer (cheeks).

Beaver Believer Waffles Cont'd

BODY AND TAIL

7. Place four chocolate wafers at each corner (hands and legs).

8. Trim the end of the third waffle and place adjacent to the head and body (tail).

Fun Fact:

Beavers' teeth are actually orange; they are herbivores with tree bark being their favorite snack.

FUN FOOD TRIVIA:

True or False.

Waffles Inspired Nike's first pair of sneakers

False

True

Answer: True

Sandwich
Crafts

- Bagel or English Muffin
- Peanut butter (or butter substitute)
- Half banana
- 2 strawberries
- Small handful of blueberries

TOOLS

- kid-safe knife

An Owlsome Sandwich

 2 servings   5 minutes

knock knock.

Who?

Who, who?

You talk like an owl!

1. Divide the bagel in half and spread peanut butter on both slices of the bagel.

2. Cut the banana into slices and put 2 slices in the center of each slice of bread (eyes).

3. Add a blueberry on top of each banana slice (pupils).

4. Cut strawberries in half and place on both sides of the bread (wings).

5. Set a tiny strawberry piece beneath the eyes (beak).

Enjoy your owl-some sandwich.

Fun Fact:

Owls can turn their heads 270 degrees. That's almost a full circle.

INGREDIENTS

- 4 bread slices
- ½ tsp. peanut butter (or butter substitute)
- ½ tsp. hazelnut spread
- ½ tsp. cream cheese
- 1 mini chocolate chip
- 1 banana
- 5 strawberries
- 8 blueberries

TOOLS

- Kid-safe knife

Fun Fact:

Wolves can run fast, reaching speeds of 38mph. Their pack can have more than 30 wolves in it.

Silly Toast

 4 servings   5 minutes

Joke:

What does a wolf do after exercising?

Huffs and puffs.

MONKEY

1. Spread hazelnut onto the bread and place 2 banana slices on top of the bread.

2. Set a blueberry in the center of each banana slice (eyes).

3. Cut the banana slice in half. Place each half on either side of the eyes (ears).

4. Cut an additional banana slice in half. Place both slices under the eyes with the flat side facing each other (mouth).

Silly Toast Cont'd

OWL

1. Spread the cream cheese on the bread.
2. Cut two banana slices and place on top of the bread (eyes).
3. Place two blueberries in the center of the banana slices (pupils).
4. Cut four strawberries vertically and align along the center and bottom of the bread (wings).

WOLF

1. Spread the cream cheese on the bread.
2. Cut two banana slices and place in the center of the bread (eyes).
3. Place two blueberries in the center of banana slices (pupils).
4. Set an additional blueberry at the bottom of the bread (nose).
5. Finally, place a strawberry slice on the top corners of the bread (ears).

BEAR

1. Spread peanut butter onto the bread.
2. Cut two banana slices and set on top of the bread (ears).
3. Place two blueberries under the banana slices (eyes).
4. Place another banana slice under the blueberries (nose).
5. Finally, set one mini chocolate chip inside the banana slice (nostrils).

Silly Toast Cont'd

Directions: Draw a picture of a wolf howling in the night.

INGREDIENTS

- 2 bread slices
- 1 tsp. mayo
- 1 slice of deli meat (or substitute)
- 1 slice of white cheese slice
- 1 cucumber half
- 2 black olives

TOOLS

- Grown-up knife
- Kid-safe knife

Cheesy Smile Sandwich

Joke:

What do chickens call bowling balls?

Eggrolls

1. Stack two slices of bread on top of each other and cut diagonally (4 triangular slices of bread will become 2 sandwiches.)

2. Use the kid-safe knife to spread mayo onto the bread.

3. Layer turkey (or substitute) halfway onto the bottom bread slice (tongue).

4. Cut cheese slice into 4-5 small rectangles (teeth) and lay onto the meat.

5. Stack final triangle bread slice on top.

6. Cut the cucumber into 2 slices and set them on top of the sandwich (eyes).

Cheesy Smile Sandwich cont'd

7. Finally, place 2 black olives on top of the cucumbers (pupils).

8. Repeat the steps for the other bread slices.

Say "cheese!" Enjoy.

(Optional: Add spinach, spring mix, mustard, and other

condiments)

Fun Fact:

Cheddar cheese is not naturally yellow. Instead, they are

usually white, off-white (and golden yellow at times.)

FUN FOOD TRIVIA:

What type of cheese is used to make mozzarella?

A. Cow's milk

B. Sheep's milk

C. Buffalo's milk

Answer: C. Buffalo's milk

Directions: Color in all the smiling faces

INGREDIENTS

- 4 slices of bread
- 4 tbsp. shredded cheddar cheese
- 4 tbsp. melted butter (divided)

TOOLS

- Rolling pin
- Small frying pan

Fun Fact:

National Grilled Cheese Sandwich Day is observed annually in the U.S. on April 12th. The world record for eating grilled cheese is 47 sandwiches in 10 minutes

Grilled Cheese Roll-Ups

 3 servings 5 minutes

Joke:

What did the cheese say to the bread? It's **grate** to meet you.

1. Trim the edges of the bread and use a rolling pin to stretch the slices.
2. Sprinkle cheese on the bread and roll up tightly.
3. Melt 2 tbsp. of butter in a pan over medium heat.
4. Melt the remaining 2 tbsp. of butter in a small bowl and dip each cheese roll-up. Then place in the pan.
5. Cook for 2 minutes on each side until crisp and golden brown.
6. Add a sheet of paper towel onto a plate and transfer each cheese roll-up onto a plate (to remove excess butter).

FUN TIP:
Serve with tomato soup, salsa, tomato sauce, or any other tasty condiments.

INGREDIENTS

- Bagel (or English Muffin)
- 1 tsp. cream cheese
- 3 strawberries
- 2 blueberries
- 2 mini chocolate chips

TOOLS

- Grown-up knife
- Kid-safe knife

Fun Fact:

Pigs are actually clean animals. They roll around in the mud to keep themselves cool. But make sure their toilet is far away from their home.

Piggy Cream Cheese Sandwich

 2 servings   3 minutes

Joke:

What do you get when you mix a pig and a dinosaur?

Jurassic pork.

1. Use kid-friendly knife to spread cream cheese on a bagel.

2. Use grown-up knife to slice one strawberry diagonally; then place slices on top of the bread (ears).

3. Cut another strawberry slice and place in the center of the bread and set 2 mini chocolate chips in the center (snout).

4. Finally, set two blueberries above the snout (eyes).

Here's a snack that will make your heart squeal. Enjoy!

What's the difference?

Piggy Cream Cheese Sandwich cont'd

Directions: Draw a picture of your favorite farm animals.

INGREDIENTS

- 2 bread slices
- 2 baby carrots
- Grapes
- Orange slice
- Cucumber slices
- 4 candy eyes

TOOLS

- Grown-up knife
- Heart-shaped mold

Blossoming Butterfly Sandwich

 4 servings  5 minutes

Tongue Twister:
Butterflies fly but a butterfly flies.

BUTTERFLY

1. Prepare the sandwich. Use a heart-shaped mold to cut out the shape.
2. Place a cucumber slice in the center of the sandwich (face). Add 2 candy eyes and a thin carrot strip under the eyes (smile).
3. Set two thin cucumber strips above the cucumber slice (antennas).
4. Slice the baby carrot vertically in half and place one half under the cucumber (body).

SUN

5. Place an orange slice along the top corner of the plate. Arrange thin carrot slices around the perimeter of the orange.

Blossoming Butterfly Sandwich Cont'd

CATERPILLAR

6. Cut a purple grape in half; place on the bottom of the plate.

7. Cut green grapes in half. Place the first grape directly behind the purple grape, one behind the other.

(Optional: Add spinach or mixed greens under the caterpillar.)

Fun Fact:

Caterpillars have 12 eyes and 6 legs.

DID YOU KNOW?

FUN FOOD TRIVIA:

60% of sandwiches sold all over the world are:

A. Ham and cheese sandwiches

B. Cheesesteak sandwiches

C. Hamburgers

Answer: C. Hamburgers

Marshmallow

Crafts

INGREDIENTS

- Crispy rice bars
- Bear-shaped crackers
- 2 tbsp. vanilla frosting
- 3-5 drops light blue food coloring
- (Optional: Gummy circle candies, Chocolate candy balls)

TOOLS

- Kid-safe knife
- Drink umbrellas

Cool Pool Bears

 3 servings  3 minutes

Joke:

How does water greet sand at the beach? It waves.

1. Mix 3 tbsp. of white frosting with 2-3 drops of blue food coloring and mix well.

2. Use a kid-friendly knife to spread the blue frosting across the top of the marshmallow crispy rice bars.

3. Have fun arranging the bears on each treat as if they are enjoying a day by the water.

Don't forget to use umbrellas for sunblock.

Fun Fact:

The first major ship to have a pool was the titanic.

3 servings 3 minutes

INGREDIENTS

- 3 jumbo marshmallows
- 2 standard marshmallows
- 6 mini marshmallows
- 6 candy eyes
- 3 brown chocolate candies
- Small handful white chocolate melting wafers

TOOLS

- Spoon
- Small bowl

Joke:

What's a polar bear's favorite food?

Ice berg-er.

1. Cut a standard-size marshmallow in half and set aside.

2. Place a small handful of white chocolate melting wafers in a bowl and melt in the microwave in 20-second intervals until melted. Watch carefully. Mix well.

3. Caution: Hot! Put a small drop of chocolate at the end of the standard-sized marshmallow and place at the end of the Jumbo Marshmallow (nose).

4. Next, put an additional drop of white chocolate on each mini marshmallow and place one on both sides of the jumbo marshmallow (ears).

Polar Bear Marshmallows Cont'd

5. Finally, use another drop of chocolate on the back of the brown chocolate candy (put chocolate on the side with the letter).

Your polar bear is ready to play in some hot chocolate!

Fun Fact:

Polar bears eat only meat: seals, reindeer, muskox, birds, and other animals.

FUN FOOD TRIVIA:

How many marshmallows to Americans eat a year?

A. 90 million pounds (approx 4,083,231 kg)

B. 2 million pounds (approx. 907,184 kg)

C. 800,000 pounds (362,873 kg)

Answer: A. 90 million pounds (approx 4,083,231 kg)

Polar Bear Marshmallows cont'd

Directions: Draw animals that live in the Arctic.

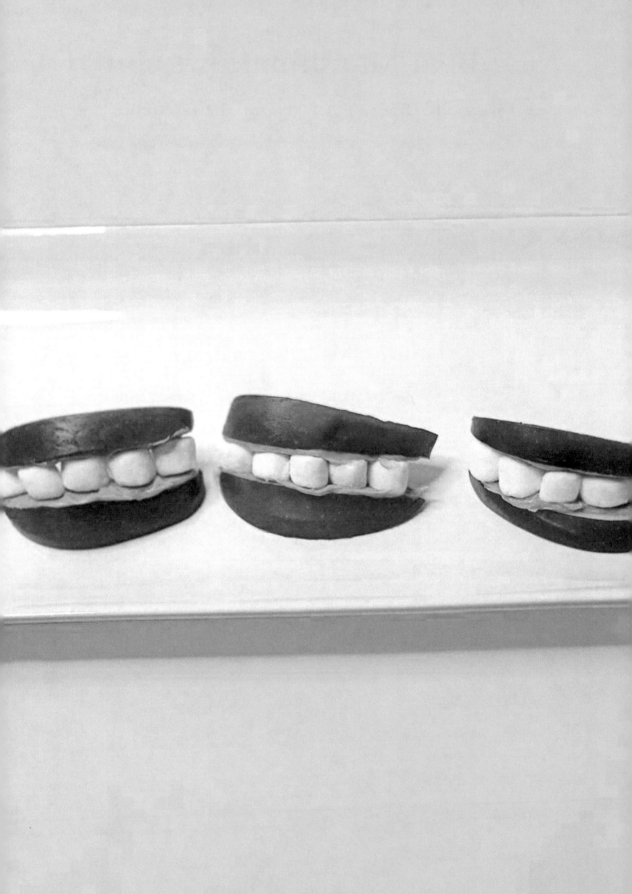

INGREDIENTS

- 1 apple half
- 15 mini marshmallows
- 2 tsp. peanut butter (or substitute)

TOOLS

- Grown-up knife
- Kid-safe knife

Apple Toothy Smiles

 3 servings  5 minutes

Joke:

Who is an apple's favorite family member? Granny.

1. Cut apple into 6 slices.
2. Spread peanut butter (or butter of choice) on each apple slice.
3. Place 5 mini marshmallows in an upright position on top of the slice.
4. Place another apple slice on top of the marshmallows (**note:** the buttered side should be facing the marshmallows so they can stick.)
5. Repeat the steps above for the remaining toothy smiles.

A snack to apple-solutely enjoy!

Fun Fact:

The first apple tree originated in Asia. Apple trees are the most widely grown tree to date. There are over 8,000 different varieties.

INGREDIENTS

- 3 jumbo marshmallows
- 5 thin pretzel sticks

TOOLS

- Black edible marker

Fun Fact:
A 60-minute massage is just as good as getting a good night's sleep of 7-8 hours.

Jumbo Spa Snowman

 2 servings   3 minutes

Joke:
What medicine do snowmen take when it's too hot? Chill pill.

1. Push one thin pretzel halfway into the center of a jumbo marshmallow.

2. Next, push the second jumbo marshmallow into the other side of the pretzel half. (You should now have two jumbo marshmallows on one pretzel stick.)

3. Use two thin pretzel sticks to connect the arms on the second jumbo marshmallow and 2 more for the legs.

4. Use a black edible marker to draw eyes on top of the marshmallow. Now your snowman is ready to enter the hot chocolate spa.

INGREDIENTS

- 4 standard marshmallows
- 8 mini marshmallows

TOOLS

- Pink edible marker
- Black edible marker
- Edible adhesive (or melting chocolate wafer)

Fun Fact:
Bunnies and Rabbits are two different words for the same animal. Hares are in the same family but different species. They are bigger with longer ears. Also, hares are solitary creatures while rabbits are social and can live with up to 20 housemates.

Mini Marshmallow Bunnies

 2 servings   3 minutes

Joke:
What medicine do snowmen take when it's too hot? Chill pill.

1. Use a black edible marker and draw eyes and mouth on the standard size marshmallow.
2. Next, use a pink edible marker to add the pink cheeks.
3. Squeeze one mini marshmallow in the center to form "bunny ears."
4. Put a small drop of edible adhesive (or melted chocolate) on the underside of the marshmallow ear and place on top of a standard size marshmallow.
5. Repeat steps 1 and 2 for the other mini marshmallows.

Your bunny is all set and ready to hop onto your plate. Enjoy!

INGREDIENTS

- 1/2 red apple
- 1/2 green apple
- 3 green grapes
- 3 purple grapes

TOOLS

- Grown-up knife
- Toothpicks

BONUS TIP:
For the ultimate quick gift, enclose stirrers in plastic wrap and pair them with a packet of hot chocolate mix.

Snowman Stirrers

 6 servings 5 minutes

Joke:

What's a snowman's friendly greeting? Have an ice day!

1. Push one marshmallow in the center, down the wooden skewer.
2. Repeat for the second and third marshmallows.
3. Next, use a black edible marker to draw the eyes and mouth.
4. Finally, use an orange edible marker to draw the nose.

Have an "ice" day! Enjoy!

Fun Fact:

Fun Fact: Japan holds the world record for the most snowmen built in an hour: 2,036.

INGREDIENTS

- Graham crackers
- 2 jumbo marshmallows
- Mini chocolate chips
- Orange sprinkles

TOOLS

- Microwave

Melted Snowman Smores

 2 servings   3 minutes

Joke:

What do campers ask marshmallows to do around the campfire?
Tell s'more jokes.

1. Place the jumbo marshmallow on top of the graham cracker and microwave for 10-15 seconds.
2. Add mini chocolate chips to form eyes and mouth.
3. Use an orange sprinkle for the nose.
4. Place a second graham cracker on top.

Fun Fact:

The original ingredient used in marshmallows (sap from mallow root) was used in Europe and Asia to treat sore throats.

Surprise: Bonus Fun

Circle All the Vegetables

Susie is very hungry. Can you help her find her sandwich?

The Baker's Coloring Page

FIND THE FRUITS

- kiwi
- blueberries
- bananas
- strawberries
- grapes
- oranges
- cucumbers
- tomatoes
- olives
- apple

F	M	S	G	R	X	N	B	H
T	K	E	M	K	H	B	L	V
O	L	I	V	E	S	K	U	X
M	C	R	W	N	H	O	E	K
A	U	R	R	I	U	R	B	J
T	C	E	G	N	U	A	E	S
O	U	B	H	V	R	N	R	A
E	M	W	J	X	M	G	R	A
S	B	A	P	P	L	E	I	N
Z	E	R	K	G	F	S	E	N
J	R	T	V	F	G	F	S	A
Z	S	S	E	P	A	R	G	B

Can you help the baked bread find the correct path to the bakery?

It's lunchtime! Help Blaze find a way to his lunch tray.

Decorate the Cakes for Arya

FIND THE INGREDIENTS

- toast
- bananas
- blueberries
- peanut butter
- hazelnut
- cream cheese
- chocolate chips

E	C	R	E	A	M	C	H	E	E	S	E	M	J	T
A	H	Q	F	R	Y	S	G	Q	X	E	W	E	U	A
T	O	A	S	T	A	E	P	X	O	I	I	L	I	S
A	C	V	I	N	P	L	N	Z	A	R	G	O	C	T
C	O	K	A	K	P	F	M	H	S	R	B	N	E	Y
O	L	N	Z	I	L	N	H	A	Z	E	L	N	U	T
S	A	U	H	W	E	E	Y	I	A	B	F	W	L	S
B	T	T	M	I	S	A	U	W	S	E	O	A	E	H
A	E	J	G	J	A	T	M	A	T	U	O	T	M	A
C	C	A	K	E	S	R	M	B	Y	L	D	E	O	R
O	H	R	G	N	H	A	Y	F	P	B	S	R	N	I
N	I	A	I	E	A	Y	Y	K	O	C	H	I	P	N
P	P	E	A	N	U	T	B	U	T	T	E	R	K	G
H	S	H	A	K	E	F	R	U	I	T	S	F	I	S

Susie is very hungry. Can you help her find her sandwich?

FIND THE INGREDIENTS TO MAKE THE PIZZA

- tomatoes
- tomato sauce
- mozzarella
- dough
- flour
- olives
- pepperoni

S	T	O	M	A	T	O	E	S	X	T
W	H	T	L	X	K	E	T	C	U	O
E	Z	P	E	I	T	A	S	T	Y	M
E	D	P	O	P	V	J	S	M	G	A
M	O	Z	Z	A	R	E	L	L	A	T
S	U	I	L	Y	S	N	S	S	G	O
P	G	A	I	U	A	R	C	A	N	S
I	H	G	V	M	U	S	T	A	R	A
N	I	B	E	O	S	N	A	C	K	U
A	J	E	L	C	E	L	E	R	Y	C
C	G	F	B	Z	S	K	B	C	A	E
H	T	D	F	K	O	H	N	K	E	P
Z	P	E	P	P	E	R	O	N	I	Q

With love, Mom

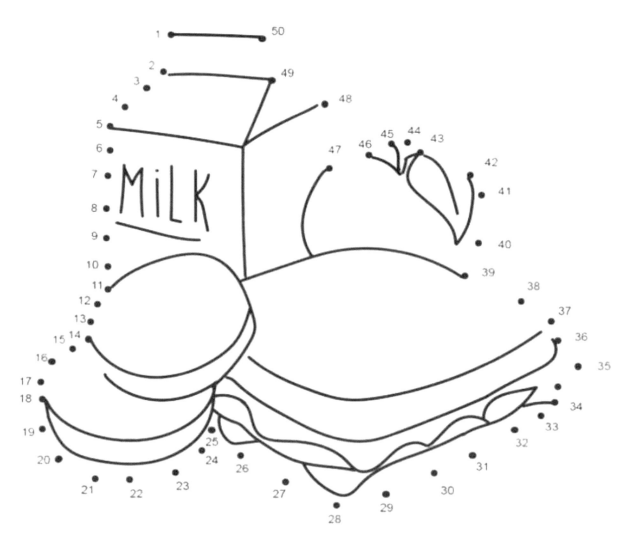

FIND THE KITCHEN TOOLS

- rolling pin
- measuring cup
- spoon
- fork
- knife
- mixing bowl
- mixer
- muffin pan
- spatula
- peeler

M	I	X	I	N	G	B	O	W	L	M
E	S	O	U	P	F	I	S	H	J	U
A	T	R	A	Y	B	O	A	R	D	F
S	S	O	U	P	F	I	S	H	J	F
U	F	B	P	M	J	S	S	V	T	I
R	O	L	L	I	N	G	P	I	N	N
I	R	S	I	X	S	Y	A	O	R	P
N	K	A	K	E	U	T	T	U	O	A
G	N	U	S	R	N	S	U	K	H	N
C	A	C	A	X	S	P	L	N	L	G
U	K	E	P	Z	I	N	A	I	Y	H
P	E	E	L	E	R	K	Q	F	Q	V
S	W	N	S	A	I	S	M	E	A	S

It is Berry Delicious!

1
2
3
4
5
6
7
8
9
10
11
12
13
14
15
16
17
18
19
20

Find a way to connect the milk and the cookies.

I Spy with my Little Eye:

- banana
- strawberry
- mango
- pineapple
- papaya
- cherry
- melon
- kiwi
- orange

FIND THE INGREDIENTS

- hot choc mix
- marshmallows
- sprinkles
- choc chips

B	M	E	H	Z	F	J	L	S	J
E	C	H	O	C	C	H	I	P	S
R	U	I	T	T	U	R	O	N	W
R	K	L	C	B	A	C	O	N	O
Y	N	F	H	P	A	S	T	A	L
J	I	S	O	C	O	O	K	Q	L
A	P	M	C	E	A	T	I	N	A
M	K	Q	M	P	A	S	T	A	M
S	P	R	I	N	K	L	E	S	H
C	M	I	X	G	K	L	D	R	S
F	L	O	U	R	W	A	T	E	R
B	U	R	G	E	R	Y	U	M	A
D	O	U	G	H	N	U	T	S	M

Find a Way Out for the Burger!

Can you help the french fries find a path to the ketchup?

Draw a line to complete the food items.

 1. cup   •

 2. milk   •

 3. chocolate •

 4. peanut   •

 5. ginger   •

 6. apple   •

 7. straw   •

 8. cheese   •

 9. oat   •

 10. pop   •

• shake

• burger

• meal

• berry

• cake

• sauce

• bread

• corn

• butter

• chip

Snacktime at school

What's for dessert?

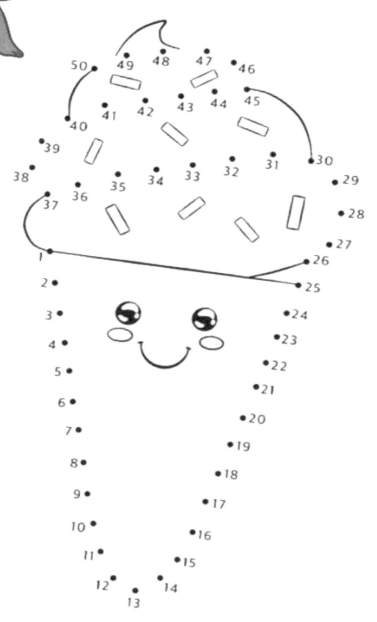

Where do I belong?

Sweet Like Corn

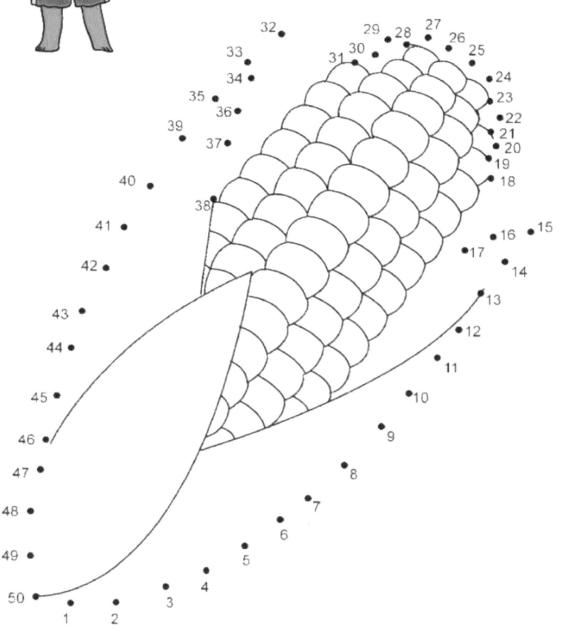

Draw a line to complete the food items.

 1. egg   •

                                      • berry

 2. flap   •

                                      • pie

 3. blue   •

                                      • cake

 4. jelly   •

                                      • water

 5. pine   •

                                      • jack

 6. cheese   •

                                      • shell

 7. lemon   •

                                      • fries

8. peach   •

                                      • melon

9. french   •

                                      • bean

 10. water   •

                                      • apple

I Spy with my Little Eye:

- sandwich
- pancake
- orange juice
- egg
- soup
- cupcake
- milk
- coffee
- bacon

What goes together?

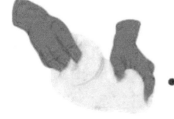

I Spy with my Little Eye:

- carrot
- potato
- pumpkin
- onion
- garlic
- mushroom
- celery
- bread
- salt

Sugar

Index

Keep the party going with done-for-you bundle deals

As a thank you for purchasing the books, we are offering bonus bundle deals only for our readers.

These offers are only found in our books and are not being offered anywhere else. Check them out below

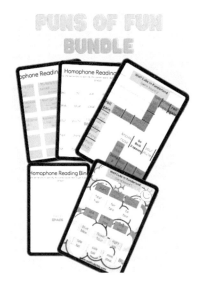

Nurture the budding comedian inside your child with the "Bundle of Laughs" Deal. This packed bundle includes a host of activities for children ages 5-9 years old. Activities range from a 50-page printable ART-ivity book and revised funny joke book for kids, to fun reading bingo games, punny game boards and more!

Visit https://jokeswolfcubchlo.com/bundle

This packed bundle includes 4 Kitchen Science Activity Books for children ages 5-9 years old plus 4 surprise bonuses. Visit the link below to get done-for-you bundles of fun for a fraction of the cost!

Visit

https://sciencewolfcubchlo.com/bundle

Made in United States
Troutdale, OR
12/12/2023

15761742R00084